THE NATURAL MEDIUM – FREESTYLING MEDIUMSHIP

DANIELLE SMITH

CONTENTS

INTRODUCTION

CHAPTER 1

CHAPTER 2

CHAPTER 3

CHAPTER 4

CHAPTER 5

CHAPTER 6

CHAPTER 7

INTRODUCTION

WHY WOULD YOU READ THIS BOOK?
AND WHAT WILL YOU GET FROM IT?

Why would you read this book? And what will you get from it?

A book on mediumship. Why would you pick that up and start reading? Well, you have made it this far and the rest will be really interesting for you. I have been practising this for a number of years and want to share my story with you. This might not follow in a straight line. A traditional story might start with the birth and then move through the life to the present day. My story is different. I will share with you the passions I have. It will share with you the way I have developed my skills – and how you can do the same too.

No two journeys are the same. This is where you need to tread carefully. Don't think that because this is the way I learned all about the spirit world that this is the exact same way it will happen for you.

Not everyone learns in the same way.

Not everyone works in the same way.

Not everyone has the same life experiences.

So, people shouldn't be trained in exactly the same way.

That can be the problem with modern mediumship training. There is too much of a one size fits all approach. One size does definitely not fit all. If you want to become your own medium, then you need to develop your own understanding and energy – not try to copy that of someone else. This book is entitled The Natural Medium – Freestyling Mediumship for a reason. That reason is I don't want you to think in the same way as anyone else. There are guidelines, exercises, stories and experiences in this book that are all designed to help you develop into your own medium. Please don't get hooked up on the exact way things happen for anyone else. Your own journey will be filled with light and hope, filled with success and failure, but it will be your own journey. The path you follow and the experiences you have along the way are just as important and far more interesting than the place you end up.

Even then, you will never stop moving, never stop learning. There is a constant development of your energy and the way you work with people. The most successful business leaders in the world work on their personal development every single day. So, why wouldn't a medium be the same? This doesn't mean that you have to become a full time medium if you don't want to, but it is best if you set aside some quality time on a regular basis to become the medium you want to be. It is such a fulfilling place to be that you will want to keep on learning every day. That's the place you will occupy. The things you learn as you read this book will get you to a certain level – it is designed to help you build your ideas and ideals – and the missing ingredient is you. Be bold, take a few risks and listen to what you are being told by the spirit world. Opening up your ears and eyes is the start, opening up your heart and mind will follow in due course.

This book will help you build your energy, so you can work with the spirit world. Too many people want to run before they can walk. It is an exciting time to start learning about the spirit world and the way that you can use your gift. But time is a major factor. It has taken me several years to reach my level of mediumship – and I am grateful for the way I have been able to develop over this period of time. Trying to do this quickly doesn't make for the best results.

Some authors to look at during your journey into mediumship that might be helpful include –

Gordon Higginson

Gordon was considered one of the best mediums of the last century and his legacy lives on today. He was showing signs of spirituality at a very early age and developed this into a wide-ranging mediumship that concentrated on helping others. He was only 12 years old when he first demonstrated his mediumship publicly and this was the start of a mediumship life that went on for more than another 60 years. He was known to provide specific evidence in his mediumship that is at the core of everything I do. Providing strong evidence is discussed at great length later in this book. Here I will only say that it is the cornerstone of an effective freestyle medium and the core of how I work.

Gordon was President of the Spiritualists National Union or SNU for an impressive 23 years and this is testament to his standing in the community. I strongly suggest you read up about Gordon Higginson and develop a good understanding of the methods of all the mediums I mention here. It is all part of becoming someone who knows about the supporting and caring side of mediumship. If you come at this from the right direction, one of trust and love, then you will go far.

The main reasons I like Gordon Higginson is that he is easy to understand and logical in the way he presents things to people. This makes him an accessible medium and one that I feel matches my own style in many ways.

Helen Duncan

Helen Duncan was a powerful medium that lived before a time where her gifts would be embraced and celebrated. She was born in Scotland in 1897, in a time where people were suspicious of anything they didn't understand. Nonetheless, Helen practiced her mediumship and was known as an excellent physical medium. The meetings she held were well-attended those who turned up were amazed at how accurate and effective she was.

She came across the church who didn't want anything to undermine the way that they taught people to believe, think and worship. This meant that Helen Duncan was labelled an evil person and was frowned upon by what was known as polite society. In 1956, she was badly injured during one of her meetings as the police barged into the room while she was in a trance state. The shock to her system was massive and she died 36 days later, never able to recover from the shock. This was a huge loss to the medium movement but here memory will live on for a very long time.

One of the things you may come across on your journey as a

freestyle medium is those that don't necessarily believe in you. Now, thankfully the times where you may be branded as evil and harassed by the church are over but there will still be some hurtful words and actions from others potentially as you become a medium. It is important to remember that not everyone thinks and loves in the same way that you do. They are coming from a place of ignorance, in the same way that the church was back in the days of Helen Duncan. Stay strong and be understanding of all others.

I really like Helen Duncan because she worked against the odds to help people in her work. Helen Duncan had so much opposition to what she did and just continued because she knew she was right. That is a powerful thing.

Estelle Roberts

Estelle Roberts was a London born medium who didn't even start to realise and develop her talent as a medium until she was in her thirties. There is nothing to say that you have to start at any age in your freestyle mediumship life. When you feel you are ready is probably the best time to go with it. Don't think that age is anything to go by – just do what you feel is right in your heart.

Estelle started her development as a medium when she visited a spiritualist church in London. There was an attempt by many there to tip tables to show that they were spiritual. Estelle tried and failed, so she walked away. It is said that as she walked away, her guide hit her on the back with the table to persuade her not to give up. That's quite a sign!

She fought hard in the 1950's to get legal recognition for

Spiritualism. She even conducted a mediumship demon-stration in the House of Commons as part of the process that saw legal recognition granted. She was a much-respected and much-loved medium who passed away in 1970, having lived for 81 years.

Estelle is symbolic of what should be in our heart when we start our path to become a medium. She was part of the movement and wanted others to accept the powers she had. This wasn't about money or fame for her in any way shape or form. It was all about helping others and developing the skills of mediums around her. Gaining legal recognition for Spiritualism doesn't feel like much of a challenge in this day and age. But nearly 70 years ago when there were some strong influences around the table, this was quite a battle. Estelle Roberts was a voice for the Spiritualism movement that was powerful and caring at the same time.

I really admire Estelle Roberts because I see a lot of myself in her. She came from a working-class background just like me. This journey is one that I identify with. In addition to this, I find Estelle easy to understand in the way she presents he work. This makes her work accessible to many people. Moving the spiritualist cause forward was her life's work and being easy to understand was a key principle in this.

Who is Danielle Smith?

I started in mediumship a few years back. You may well have seen one of my shows, watched me on You Tube or seen one of my Facebook Live sessions.

And it started with humble beginnings. I was born and raised in Stanley in County Durham. From a working-class background, with my mother working in retail and my father an engineer, I didn't see a future where I was in high demand for my skills as a medium – and now publishing her my book to help others on their freestyle medium journey. I moved into nursing as a career, always ready to help others. It has been my life's calling to look after other people and this now transcends my life as a medium, mother, friend and human being.

I love to travel and see what the world has to offer. There is so much out there that travelling is in my blood. Wherever I am, I like to party. I have spent time with some of the more colourful people in life and enjoy this lifestyle – who doesn't?

But behind all of this lives a person who lives by certain characteristics –

Being no nonsense

Someone who is easy to relate to

I am intensely truthful and am not afraid to speak up

I love to meet new people and listen to what they have to say about the world

An impulsive person who sees things and wants to know more about them

All of these characteristics have come together to deliver someone who helps others. I love to see the happiness on the faces of people that I work with. It gives me the most amazing feeling in the world. And long may it continue...

At the end of all of this is a normal person who has an amazing ability to connect to the spirit world. And now I am sharing that gift with you.

Here are the answers to some questions relating to the basics of mediumship

This section of the book is put in early for one reason – there are far too many myths out there associated with mediumship. You should know from the start that there are certain things you will and will not be expected to do as a medium. The freestyle mediumship that I teach is one that allows you to learn in your own time and your own way. That is the beauty of it. You will find your own path and become the medium you are meant to be with a little guidance and support. So, here are some of the questions that will set the scene for you and put you on the right path to becoming and effective medium -

Will I need to go into a trance to become an effective medium?

This is a great question and throws up some really interesting areas for discussion. There is a short answer, but it isn't anywhere near as stimulating as understanding what this is all about in terms of your body and mind. There are four main stages of sleep – and these are linked to your brain waves. Understanding brain waves will help you to alter your state of consciousness. This is where you can start to tap into abilities that you maybe didn't know existed until reading this book. Let's take a look in a little detail at what the four main brain wave states are and how they can affect you –

Beta Brain Waves are those that are linked to our conscious mind and the way we think when awake. They cycle between 14 and 30 times per second and connect to normal waking activity – the everyday. Beta brain waves are focused on the events happening right around us and all of the senses these events evoke. The stimulation from the outside world is so strong in these brain waves that we don't really connect to our spiritual thoughts. They just don't have a chance to make headway.

There are many people out there that only live in a world where they work with beta brain waves. Some can slip into another state (we will look at these next) and find this an uncomfortable place to be. They quickly bring themselves back into the 'real world' and run away from the inner thoughts and reflection that another state might being them. They turn on the TV, get their phone out or talk to someone rather than take the time to reflect on their inner self. You tend to find people that live along these lines are reasonably unhappy with their self and don't want to connect with it in any way shape or form. It is easier to hide from it than to do anything about it. They may be aware of connections to something beyond the everyday noise but don't acknowledge it or want anything to do with it.

<u>Alpha Brain Waves</u> are a more aware stat of mind and these tend to oscillate at between 8 and 13 cycles per second. You can feel from that drop in cycles that they are a calmer and more grounded set of brain waves than Beta Brain Waves. This is far more focused and far more introspective than anything created in the beta mind state.

Alpha Brain Waves occur in calming and relaxing places such as the bath or in bed – basically when we are most relaxed and open to thinking about ourselves and the position we occupy in the world. We are probably most aware of Alpha Brain Waves when they are not there at all – laid in bed at night trying to get to sleep when our mind is firing questions and answers left, right and centre. We try as much as we can to silence the brain and get some rest. This is the Beta Brain Waves taking over and giving you all of the information they think you need. But that is the time to switch off from Beta and accept the Alpha in your life! Once you let the inner talk and noise disappear then you will be amazed at the things that start to come your way.

You should try to access this state of mind when you are developing your freestyle mediumship. It is the state where you can gain observations about yourself and others. We don't as a rule access this state anywhere near enough, so try to find a space where you are not disturbed and not distracted. This is the space that will help you to gather your thoughts. If you want to focus in something specific, then you can do this through Alpha Brain Waves by zoning out of everything else and spending your time just concentrating on this one thing to the exclusion of everything else.

Alpha Brain Waves are not only accessed when you are lying down with your eyes closed or sat in the bath with the door locked and a few candles burning. They can be connected to when you are walking or even carrying out daily chores. It is that point where you switch off to what you are doing and think about something far deeper. It is when you don't need your full attention to do something that you can often zone out and find that you have been thinking about something else altogether. I suppose it is what we were told was daydreaming when we were kids in many ways. It is about connecting to something more spiritual and internal than the thing we have sat right in front of us.

<u>Theta Brain Waves</u> are the next level in brain waves after Alpha and these only oscillate at around 4 to 5 cycles per second. This is the brain waves that we can readily associate with deep meditation and can open up our mind to things that Alpha Brain Waves just can't access. Theta Brain Waves can rise above simple space and time. They are perfect for gaining information from deep within or without you and allow you to develop remote perceptions about the world around you and yourself too.

We are moving along the brain waves and always getting closer to our source self. There is a pure self at the core of our being and these different brain waves help us to connect with this. Theta Brain Waves are almost completely inward and don't connect to or engage with the outside world. And there is another level of unconscious mind to consider –

<u>Delta Brain Waves</u> are the unconscious mind at its peak (but can also be connected to the super-conscious mind) and oscillate at less than 4 cycles per second. As you can see, we have got to fewer and fewer cycles per second as we have moved along this list of brain waves. These are actually the kind of brain waves you would associate with someone in a coma. But this isn't the only way that these operate – deep sleep and profound states of meditation are shown to have Delta Brain Waves at their centre. Delta states are essential to the way the brain recovers from each and every day, but the information that is passed in this state doesn't really come back with us into consciousness. The memory of the Delta state is only fleeting and isn't something that most can relay into words that make any sense. You can access Delta Brain Waves through guided meditation, but it is more easily reached in the deepest sleep of our normal sleep cycle.

Put simply – your everyday life is lived in Beta, the last time you found yourself daydreaming you were in Alpha, the last dream you remember was from your Theta and the last time you were sure you had a dream but can't remember it is Delta.

Now all of these are a part of everyday life, but you need to move away from Beta Brain Waves at least several times per day and for some time to develop your mediumship. Living in the Beta where all the noise of the world around you exists does nothing for your development as a freestyle medium. The higher state you can enter, the better it will be for your spiritual development. Think about how you can get to a place where you can access Alpha Brain Waves several times per day and have the tools to get into Theta Brain Waves when you need it.

Do spirits know everything?

This is another great question. The spirit that you connect to only has a certain amount of intelligence and support that they can give you. This is the same level of intelligence that they had when they were on earth. Spirits, like people, can't suddenly gain a stack of knowledge just because they are in the spirit world. They need to learn like the rest of us. Some spirits come back and learn again while others stay as they are for the rest of time.

A spirit doesn't know everything just because they are a spirit. They can choose to learn and become better – and this will obviously help you too. They can learn either in the spirit world or back here on the mortal plain if they choose. Development isn't something that just stops when a spirit moves from a mortal body to the spirit world. It can continue be a part of the spirit. Intelligence is only as much as the spirit has experienced and been able to gather and learn. It isn't an 'automatic upgrade' when they pass to the spirit world.

Who will be my guide?

Another really interesting question that has a number of answers. It is said that everyone is assigned a spirit guide at birth. This principle states that you will have someone looking over you from the moment you are born onto this planet. The choice is yours as to whether you choose to accept this guide or not.

Your guide may not be with you for the long haul. This isn't a reflection on your ability as a medium or their loyalty as a spirit guide. They may only have the experience and intelligence to get you part of the way before they pass you over to someone else more suited to take you on t the next part of the journey. If you view all of this as a journey, then you will see why you may need more than one guide for the different parts of that journey our life and mediumship will throw up.

With both of these scenarios, there is a degree of give and take that has to happen in the relationship you develop with your spirit guide. It isn't about just accepting the spirit guide that you have been connected with. You have to be sure about this guide and be in a position of trust and safety with them. There are certain questions that you should ask in this process –

<u>Who are you?</u> This is probably the most important question

of all to ask. You want a spirit guide that you can connect to and believe in. So, finding out who someone is will help you on the road to becoming the freestyle medium that you are meant to be.

Where are you from? This is another consideration you should make before you accept a spirit guide to help you on your path. If you don't know where someone is from and what they are all about then you can't really make a decision that you can back with any real confidence. Find out where your spirit guide is from to see if you have the things in common that will help you make the most of this relationship.

What is your back story? Now we are getting to the juicy bits! The back story of your spirit guide will tell you a lot about how well you could work together in the future. This is about seeing the connections you have, the way you both see the world and how you can develop together. If you find out the back story, then you will have a good idea about the person and what they can provide you. There will be certain needs you have in all of this – you should look for a spirit guide that can help fill in the blanks you have in this area.

How long have you been in the light? This is another excellent question that will help you establish the experience your spirit guide has. If this is all really new to you then you will want to look for an experienced spirit guide that will answer a lot of your questions and help you become as good as you want as a freestyle medium. If your spirit guide hasn't been in the light for very long, then you might not get the support you need on this path.

In short, you should ask questions – far too many people

just accept the spirit guide they have been given without finding out of they are a suitable match. This isn't about being ungrateful or picky. This is an important part of the process. The spirit guide won't leave you unless you let them go. If they are not the right spirit guide for you then don't be afraid to make that decision and begin the search for the right one.

But the fact is that not everyone will know their guide. They will feel the support and guidance but don't develop what we would equate to a personal relationship with a guide.

And do you know what? This is perfectly OK. You don't have to know your guide to be a fantastic freestyle medium. So, don't be afraid if this happens to you. It doesn't stop you carrying out any of the techniques found in this book. You will be able to do everything we discuss here and much more.

Don't be afraid or worried if you don't get to know your guide. You can still be a great medium.

Is a medium always successful?

There is a short answer to this – no, absolutely not! It isn't the case that the medium has the spirit world connected all the time and can just tap into the answers needed for someone. There are so many variables in this equation that you cannot guarantee success. And what you may define as success might not look like success to the person you are working with. We will look at this in some more depth as the book goes on as there are some quite defined reasons why a medium might not achieve success on any given day. For this part of the book think about the factors that might contribute to success or otherwise in your job. You may be tired, not have had enough sleep, feel hungry or just not connect in some way on any given day. It is the same with mediumship. Don't give yourself a hard time if this happens. It's just part of being a freestyle medium. Be honest with people and they will work with you.

What does the rest of the book cover?

You might have some ideas about what this book will cover. And some of these ideas will be perfect. I want you to read with the spirit of mediumship in mind. But I suggest you walk through it with an open mind – a completely open mind. Having a set agenda of what you will discover with this book might lead you to miss certain things when reading. You should always have a few things you want to achieve, and we will go through this in more detail in the next section, but never close your mind to the wonders of the universe. The spirit plain is a place where you have complete free will and can make decisions that shape your future. The same is true here on earth. Don't create a narrow construct of your learning. It will only lead you to regret your path at a later point in time. The more open you are now, the more open you will be when new experiences come your way. If you are looking in the other direction, then you will mis the things that can change your life for the better. That's pretty much the case for every aspect of life anyway.

This book may ask as many questions as it answers in your mind. Don't worry about that at all. Questions are the things that prompt us to find out more. They are the things that spark the imagination and put us on the road to discovery. You won't know all of the answers when you have finished reading this book anyway. The thing you have to go out there and do is to practice, learn and develop. There will be exercises and prompts in the book but much of this will be your own unique experience as you go along. Most, if not all, of the factors in your path will have been experienced by others before – but not all of the factors in the order you experience them. This is what makes mediumship such a rewarding and supportive thing to learn. Others will be able to share with you the experiences they have had. You can come together and work through all of this in a supportive environment that feels like being part of a family.

This isn't one of those books that you might read from cover to cover in one sitting. It's just not designed in that way. This book will be one that you read a little, go away to think and then take some steps towards your mediumship goals.

I suggest you use it in this way. If you are unsure about how things will go then this is perfect for you. Read a little, try it out and then build on it with the next section.

Stop now and think about what you want from the book

This book is designed to get you on track with your freestyle mediumship. But one of the things that you need to consider from the very start is why you want to learn more about mediumship and potentially become a medium. One of the things I hear all the time from people is that they want to be a medium because they can make a lot of money from it. This really is the wrong idea and if you are reading this book to make a stack of cash then I suggest you stop and think about this before you read any further. You can make money from this but the quest to earn can lead you in the wrong direction.

This book is a guide to get you on the right path. It is designed to develop your skills as a medium in a freestyle way. That means you adapt to the situations in front of you, learn in a more fluid manner and become the medium you are meant to be.

But that is all about you helping yourself, helping others and helping the movement – not about getting your hands on money.

People will see through your motives if they are not pure. The best professional musicians learn their art, practice what they do and become the best. They don't get into the music because of the money. They get into it for the love of the art. They get into it because they love to make other people happy. The sight of thousands of smiling faces and the sound of them singing back their song at a gig is an amazing feeling for a musician.

The same applies with your mediumship. You should be doing it because you want to carry on the movement and be a part of it. You should always follow your heart and do something you love. The sight of people filling up with joy because you have been able to connect them with a loved one is what you should be in this for. The money that comes with that is incidental in many cases. You will fill with joy and love for the people you work with.

If you don't yet know what you want from this book, then you might not get as much from it as you can. I suggest you go into this with your eyes open. This has been an introduction and from here we will go deeper into the world of a medium. Know what you want, and you will stand a much better chance of achieving it.

CHAPTER 1

THE DIFFERENCE BETWEEN A PSYCHIC
AND A MEDIUM

WHAT ARE THE MAIN DIFFERENCES
BETWEEN A PSYCHIC AND A MEDIUM?

The difference between a psychic and a medium

The difference between a psychic and a medium can be confusing. This is because both disciplines have similarities and as such, can overlap in the way in which they are practiced. In order to clarify these differences, we outline here the difference between a psychic and a medium. We then go on to explore these differences in more detail. And finally, we finish off by outlining why these differences really matter.

What is the definitional difference between a psychic and a medium?

Psychic. A psychic uses information that they perceive from a client. And this is achieved through a number of techniques. Such as clairaudient (perceptive hearing), clairvoyant (perceptive seeing), clairsentient (perceptive sensing and feeling), and claircognizant (perceptive knowing) All of this information is put together to provide a clear and accurate reading and furthermore, is used to build a bigger picture of the persons spirit. It is true to say that each and every human being will have at least one of these abilities. As such, an individual that is developing their psychic abilities either has an innate ability to do this. Or alternatively, have honed their skill. In the same way that continual practice while learning a musical instrument makes you better and better over time.

Medium. Unlike a psychic who perceives information from a client, a medium instead receives this information. Which is done alongside psychic interpretation of clients. Like psychics, practice of this skill only makes the individual develop even further. Particularly a greater emphasis on information contained within the spiritual world, rather than the physical world.

What are the main differences between a psychic and a medium?

The tools that are used between mediums and psychic readers are different. Mediums tend to use visual information to describe to their client's personal things by using information such as images and descriptions of events. Contrastingly, psychics do not work towards any set of rules. And as such, they are capable of working with things such as tarot cards, astrological charts or palm reading.

Psychics tune into the vibrational energy of a human being so that they can gather specific information about their client. As such, this allows the psychic to determine things that may have happened in the clients past. Or things that may occur in their present or future. Contrastingly, a medium communicates with spirits. An important thing to remember here is that mediums possess psychic abilities. However, not all psychics have this ability. As such, the field of mediumship is considered to be higher developed in terms of psychic development.

It is possible for psychics and mediums to have certain preferences about where they work, as this may affect their comfort greatly. As well as the types of object they work with. The ability for a psychic to receive information from clients can vary. Some are very good at it whereas others develop this skill over time, allowing them to communicate better with spirits.

There is a general perception that psychic mediums are more credible than psychic readers. One possible reason for this is the way they are perceived by the media. Particularly, the dominant coverage of mediums over lesser coverage of readers. Additionally, afterlife is a common part of many religions. And as such, this can appeal to such people more. As opposed to the practices of psychics who use things such as palm reading. Which are sometimes viewed by the general public as being less credible.

Similar to the above, psychics are generally more in the public eye, being the star guests of many TV appearances and also being highly engaging with their audiences. They are more commonly viewed as 'celebrities' by the general public and may even have written a book. In comparison, psychic readers do not have as much exposure as this and may be seen as being more solitary.

Mediums generally charge higher fees for their clients that psychics. This is mainly because of the reasons I have already mentioned above, that they are more within the public eye and generally better engaged with their audiences. Some psychics charge a fairly low rate per minute. Whereas in contrast, mediums generally charge a much higher fee for a longer meeting.

Why do these differences matter?

Psychics perceive information from various different sources to help build a picture of that person's spirit. Mediums receive this information and interpret psychic information of the client. As such, a greater emphasis is placed on receiving information from the spiritual world rather than the physical one.

To work out whether you would benefit from seeing either a psychic or a medium, we have created a summary below to help you.

- Are you keen to use visual information in order to delve further into personal events in your life? Or would you prefer to work alongside someone that tends to work to not set ritual, instead using techniques such as palm reading, astrological charts or tarot cards?
- Would you like someone to tap into your vibrational energy to find out more about you, specifically what happened in the past and present, or what could happen in the future? Or are you looking for someone that can communicate with your spirit and possibly even exercise psychic abilities?
- Do you have any limitations on the types of environments you could attend to see a psychic or medium?
- Does your religion promote life after death, or are you interested in this concept? Or alternatively, are you interested in palm reading?
- Do you have a certain budget?

All in all, a psychic doesn't have the same level of interaction with the spirit world as a medium. While a medium will have someone specific they are engaging with, a psychic reads energy. This means that they see the energy in a kind of 3-dimensional way. They can feel energy and then work with it. An example might be –

"I have a 5 foot 2 inch grandmother here, who can take this?"

The fact that many people will have a small grandmother opens up the possibility of someone in the room being able to make that connection. The psychic will get that initial connection, that initial energy and then try to work with that based on the little information they have.

The medium will work in a more 4-dimensional way. They will have that connection with someone in the spirit world and use that connection to be told certain specific things about the person they are sitting with. If there is little detail in the first piece of information, as with the 5 foot 2 grandmother above, then they will go back for more information. They can ask their spirit guide (or simply listen) and find out some specific information that will attach this person to a single other person in the room. Not waiting for people to come forward and then working with that, the medium instead might say –

"And this 5 foot 2 inch grandmother has half of her left leg missing."

All of a sudden, we have a direct connection to someone in the room and the connection is deep and meaningful. We will look at the evidence levels that this brings about in more detail later in the book, but for now you can start to see how this comes from the difference between the psychic and the medium.

A second and really important difference between a medium and a psychic relates to the timeline of the spirit world. The medium will be able to provide proof that the soul continues after death. The fact that as a medium you are being guided by someone from the spirit world means you have access to this proof. But it needs to be put in a way that means something to the person on the earth plane that you are speaking to. The soul never dies because it is based in love. Love continues past the end of the mortal life. It is this very idea that the medium can work with in a way that a psychic cannot. As the psychic works with energy and not a guide, they can only feel the energy that is available around you. Now this may be something they can vaguely work with, but it is nowhere near the same thing as the way a medium works. I'm sure you have already seen this, but the psychic will work with the way you feel about someone, the energy that you are giving off. This means they don't get the evidence that the soul continues after life. They are not able to prove the existence of love beyond the mortal realm. They can just feel the love and energy that you give off.

What is the difference between mediumship clairvoyance and psychic clairvoyance?

Psychic clairvoyance

A psychic is someone who receives information from a source. And works between this and another person. They can connect with the divine source to provide someone with information, guidance and support at present.

And can interpret information provided by the divine source. Resultantly, all mediums have some level of psychic ability. Which are used to deliver a message to an individual. Mediums are also psychic. But this doesn't always occur the other way around. For example, a medium can gather information from someone using their clairaudient ability. However, this does not involve the physical body.

So, in short, a medium is someone who is merely conveying information between two points of interest. There are many information sources mediums can gather messages from. Such as loved ones that have passed away, angels and spirit guides.

Mediumship clairvoyance

Psychics receive information by connecting with a spirit. In order to achieve this, a shift in focus occurs. i.e. from information in the physical world to information in the spiritual world.

CHAPTER 2

BUILDING TRUST WITH PEOPLE

HOW YOU GET THE TRUST OF THOSE YOU WORK WITH

How you get the trust of those you work with

Let the spirit world be your guide in all of this. You need to give a large piece of control over to your spirit guide and trust that they know what they are doing. Let them guide you to show you what is out there, not attempt to get them to do what you want them to do. They are a free spirit and able to make their own choices and come to their own decisions. Let them talk freely and pay attention to what they have to say. This will be the guide you need to start to make those connections between the spirit plain and the world we live in. If it is appropriate and important then ask a question. Your spirit guide won't mind that at all. But only ask questions if they are appropriate and important. Asking lots of questions in the early days is a natural thing and you might feel like you want to go really deep with your guide straight away. This probably isn't the way to go. You should listen far more than you question, as your spirit guide will know how to help you.

Trust is at the core of everything you do in life.

If people don't trust you then you won't go very far at all as a medium. The way we gain trust is to be honest with the people you encounter. Don't ever be tempted to 'fill in the blanks' or give something over to the person you are speaking to that you have made up. There are so many ways that you can build trust. The time you spend with others is valuable and giving this time will help you develop your skills and confidence.

But none of these acts as quickly as something that works in the opposite direction – destroying trust. Acting in a dishonest or dysfunctional way will make trust in what you do dissipate overnight. The word will work its way around people in your community (this happens even more quickly than ever with social media and text messaging) and you will lose all of that hard-earned trust built up over time. Don't be tempted to take shortcuts or do things that are not 100% true to what you do. I can't label this point enough – it is vitally important.

But before you achieve this, you need the trust of two people

1. yourself
2. your spirit guide

These are the most important people to build trust with in the first place. You need to be able to trust the things that you are hearing, seeing and feeling. If you don't trust that (acceptance is the first step here) then you can't begin to pass this on to other people with any confidence.

A big step in this is to understand your own energy. This comes from meditation and sitting in the power. If you don't know your own energy, then you won't be able to recognise another energy in your life. Meditation allows you the chance to listen to yourself and be alone with just your energy. Understand what that feels like in different times of the day and in different mind states. If you know what your energy is then you will be able easily spot another energy in your presence.

Sitting in the power is all about being in the right state to receive from the spirit world. Rather than the calm, almost trance-like state you are in for meditation, sitting in the power taps into a certain energy. Start in a relaxed state, because you need an open mind to be able to receive from the spirit world.

You need to work with your spirit guide to get in the right place with them too. This is a relationship that will probably last for a long period of time, so you need to be on the same page.

Building trust with your spirit guide might take a little time. But there are some simple steps you can take to get yourself in the right place here.

Ask for a sign. Tell your spirit guide that you want to see a sign that they are who they say they are and that they are working with you. Ask for something simple but precise such as, "send me a penny within the next 3 hours." If you receive this sign, then this will put you and your guide in the right place to work together.

Or, you could ask, "is the phone going to ring soon?" Will it be a male or a female that will ring?" All of the ways in which you can test your relationship with your spirit guide will allow you to build up an understanding and strength. Believe me, you will need it as time goes on!

Without that trust, you can't hope to build those connections with the people in the world around you.

For me, I have learned to trust the signs. I've always tried to second guess what was coming – it's part of my nature! I still get excited now when I sit with someone and think about what might happen. It took me a little while to get used to trusting the signs. Before that I would receive information from the spirit world and maybe question what it meant or think twice about whether it might be relevant. Over time I have learned to trust what I was being shown and build on it from there. This will happen to you too.

When you trust yourself, there is a confidence to your work. I sat with a lady once for a reading. She had been desperate to hear from her mother. She had seen countless other mediums in search for a message from her dear Mam. Nothing. She hadn't made a connection in over 25 years of trying. When she came to me, she wasn't even the person there for the sitting. That was her friend. But this lady's Mam came through and left her a message. It was when the lady was ready and when the spirit felt she was in the right place to receive this information.

That's where your confidence and trust in all of the things around you really comes to the fore. Think about the way that you can communicate and how calm you can be. This is how you build a level of trust with yourself, your spirit guide and the people that will take you forward as a medium.

Building an idea of how to get your message across

Communication is one of the tools of the freestyle medium that will transform the way you engage with others. You can have all of the medium skills in the world, but unless you can engage with people, they won't be worth a thing. The way that you connect with both the spirit world and the real world can have a huge impact on the way that your message is received.

I would suggest that you work on this part of your freestyle mediumship as much as becoming a medium. There are loads of books out there on being an effective communicator, so think about what this actually means for you. It might be –

- Making the small talk at the beginning of a meeting to put the other person at ease
- Listening to and asking the right questions of your spirit guide
- Translating the information you are given in the right way so it means something to the person you are sitting with
- Understanding and answering the questions you are asked
- Working in different styles with a diverse range of people
- Promoting yourself as a medium to others in order to practice your mediumship

Each of these needs to be delivered in an effective and easy to understand manner. The way that you work with people will be defined by the communication style you develop.

The better you become at each of these, the better you will be received by the people you work with.

Having said this, don't try to be something that you are not. There are too many people in this world that try to become something that isn't natural. This will jar with others and will stand out like a sore thumb. Your style should be a natural thing that comes from your heart – not something that has been manufactured because you want to be seen as anything other than exactly who you are.

What trust means to you and your people

I can't say this enough – trust opens doors for you.

The way that you work with others must be embedded in an all-encompassing trust. People will gravitate to someone that they trust. Think abut all you do in terms of becoming a freestyle medium. There is a journey – people will accept that. The day after you decide to develop as a medium, you won't be the complete article. Those around you will accept that. You must accept that of yourself.

Honesty starts with telling people what you are all about. There is a phrase in business that says, "people buy people." Now, we've spoken about the need to be in this for all the right reasons, so I sometimes hesitate using business terms, but there is an undeniable truth in this phrase. People will come to you as a medium because they like you as a person. So, let them in. Let them get to know you. It's the very least you can offer because you are going to need them to return the favour. You want to get to know them.

Your word is your bond (another phrase borrowed from the wider world) and when you are a medium, your word is the tool that you will find yourself using most of all.

The words that you put together carry a strong meaning – so make sure they are used without confusion or misunderstanding. The people who need to trust the words that come out of your mouth will thank you for it.

There will be times where you have to deliver difficult or upsetting communications. Don't ever be afraid to do it. The information that you get from your spirit guide is something precious and can make a huge difference to the lives of the people you are sitting with. You should pass on this information with a style that is both natural to you and caring to them.

Shying away from delivering this information because you believe it might be upsetting feels wrong. You will get more and more used to this as time goes by. The feedback you get from others as you become a more accomplished freestyle medium will show you that giving this information over in the right manner is comforting in the long run even if it might be a little upsetting in the immediate situation. And all of this links into free will. But what is free will?

Free will?

Some people hold the belief that the future can be predicted with incredible accuracy. In reality however, this is not the case. And this is because human beings can exercise free will.

Everyone around the world has the right to exercise their own free will. Free will can be defined as "the ability for every human being to exercise personal choice outside the control of forces both divine and physical".

To make this definition more straightforward to understand, every human being has a choice. And as such, events in our lives are not laid out for us. Moreover, any choices that we make can ultimately result in a particular outcome. And specifically, the actions that we make can affect outcomes of any psychic readings we might have.

Try and imagine a world without free will. We would essentially, be living in a world where our life would be clearly set out in front of us. Almost like a puppet on a string. If this was true, it would leave us little in the way of experiencing

everything life has to offer. And ultimately, life would probably be very dull.

Why is free will important?

Free will can possibly affect relationships. Although a
psychic prediction can reveal specific information about
your life, it is free will that will ultimately determine this. As
such, if something is part of your destiny, it will definitely
happen.

Free will is not the same as intuition. As such, if our intuition tells us not to do something, this is part of our free will.

What significance does this have for mediumship?

Sometimes, predictions made in psychic readings come
true. However, you may wonder why some predictions
become true whereas others don't? Someone able to make
psychic predictions can sense the direction you are going to
take. However, your own free will can change this at any
time. However, people you are involved in can also have the
power to do this. Ultimately helping change the overall
outcome.

It is right to say that not all predictions made by a psychic
will become a reality. However, psychics do indicate the
energy you give off. And as such, can make suggestions as to
which path in life may suit you best.

So, when you decide to choose a psychic, look out for one
that will not make predictions that are set in stone. Instead,
choose one that will reveal the outcomes of choosing one
path over the other.

The psychic should indicate possibilities to the client so that they can make use of their own free will rather than be dictated to.

However ultimately, if you would just like some predictions, this is entirely your choice.

CHAPTER 3

THE 7 PRINCIPLES OF SPIRITUALISM

WHAT ARE THE PRINCIPLES?

What are the principles?

The basis of SNU spiritualism is built upon the foundation of The Seven Principles. The Seven Principles help Spiritualists to not only navigate their journeys, both spiritually and human, but to also combine these journeys. These principles were originally created by Emma Hardinge Britten, a well-known medium. And for individuals who have committed to Spiritualism for their religion, these principles will be used in their everyday lives.

The Fatherhood of God

The universe is surrounded by creative forces at every turn and everywhere we look. And such creative forces help 'make the world go round'. Nature is indeed an incredibly vast field. So vast in fact that it would be impossible to talk in depth about it here. And we as individuals of the Earth can begin to learn in more detail the laws associated with cause and effect. Which describes the relationships between actions and events, further connecting these processes together. These laws are occurring around us all the time. Certain forces and energies are responsible for the many forms of life that populate the Earth today, in addition to the creation of the entire universe. The creation of life forms continues today and furthermore, will do so long into the future. The effects of this are highly visible as we look around and explore our surroundings. And in a much wider context, our planet as well. We can even go so far as to identify living things in outer space. One such way that evidence of this is provided is through the breath-taking images taken by the Hubble telescope. God is the ultimate creative force. Evident in all living things and existing everywhere. God exists in ways that are both visible to the human eye, and even indirectly. In ways that the human eye cannot see. Because god created our life, it is essential that we acknowledge him as our father. Ultimately, we should acknowledge god as the ultimate creator of life itself.

The Brotherhood of Man

As human beings, we all come from the same life source. And this is regardless of where we are from or our background. As such, the world can be viewed as one large global community. Or perhaps even one large family. Another way that this could be described, is that humanity can also be seen as being part of a brotherhood. But what exactly is a brotherhood you may be asking? Well it describes a community that provides both mutual comfort and support for all its members. As such, all members are from a mutual divine family. Which is a family that originated from god. Because we all derive from the same human family, we have a duty to look out for each other. And as part of this, we need to try and understand the needs of others. To make sure that we are providing a service amongst our fellow man. Life is always about balance. As such, as well as giving back to others by helping them at times of need, we also need to accept that when we are in times of need ourselves, we should gracefully and thankfully accept this help from our fellow man. Helping us work towards achieving the ultimate balance within our lives.

The Communion of Spirits and the Ministry of Angels

The Communion of Spirits and the Ministry of Angels are considered an incredibly important principle by many spiritualists. The concept of life after death is common in many types of religion and exists in many forms. For example, reincarnation, resurrection, rebirth and immortality. However, it is demonstrated particularly effectively by the religion of Spiritualism. As such, the religion of spiritualism shows practically, that communication with the afterlife, particularly spirits, does occur. Specifically, there are special places designed for this type of communication with the afterlife. And these are spiritualist churches and centres. These places provide opportunities for people to speak to their former friends and relatives. And as such, those that are in spirit form, can communicate with their loved ones. This helps to offer reassurance and compassion in our current welfare. Spirituality is so important, that dedicated individuals exist out there who dedicate their time to the wellbeing of other people. One example of such people is Maurice Barbanell who offers both teachings and inspiration to the people. However, there are other types of spirits that exist. For example, people who are members of the healing ministry.

The Continuous Existence of the Human Soul

It is commonly known that the creation of matter and energy or furthermore, the destruction of it, is an impossibility. And although this fact is particularly well known within the scientific community, it is still continually being proved by a significant body of scientific research. Whether we choose to accept these facts or not (and really there is no valid reason why we should not at the present time) it is essential for the human race to know when this energy will no longer be viable. One potential outcome could be that the energy simply changes into another form. Similar principles can be applied to that of the concept of spirit. Which can similarly be viewed as an indestructible force. As you will already realise, the human body will not operate for the rest of time. It is an organic entity which will eventually die. However, when the physical body can no longer exist, the spirit will still remain and will enter our world in different ways. This phenomena is known as the spiritual world. There are two different versions of ourselves. A physical version and a spiritual version. Essentially, the spiritual body is somewhat of a copy of our physical existence, However the formation of it is much finer. Although we are all human beings, and all have similarities, it is possible for us to progressively change by investing into ourselves.

Personal Responsibility

It is essential for an individual that has committed a deed or wrongful thought to accept full responsibility for this. And this is the case, no matter which area of our lives we have done this in. As human beings, we should be 100% responsible for our own spiritual development. Other people should not be responsible for our own spiritual development, only us. However, if we allow other people to control this, it will inevitably take effect. Whether we like this or not. The beauty of life is that at every turn, we are free to make our own decisions. I.e. exercise our right to utilise our own free will when we see fit. Ultimately, we are able to determine what is right and what is wrong in terms of our own spirituality. And in a wider context, we must take full responsibility for our thoughts, deeds and words. Because these can affect not only ourselves, but others too.

Compensation and Retribution Hereafter for all the Good and Evil Deeds done on Earth

You may be familiar with the phrase 'what goes around comes around'. Which generally refers to the actions or behaviours someone commits. Which eventually will make their way back to that person either directly or indirectly. A common example seen in everyday life is if you treat other people badly. By being rude and disrespectful to others, you cannot expect in return for people to be courteous and pleasant with you. And it is quite clear that this happens not only in the spiritual world, but very much in the physical world as well. So much, in fact that you may witness this on a day to day basis. Perhaps in your place of work or even in your own home with family members. Individuals should always make an attempt to make good situations that have been negatively impacted by themselves. And subsequently have caused problems for themselves and others. Ultimately, the time period in which we have to achieve this is limited. Make sure that within your lifetime, you can at least say that you made every effort to put right the wrongs that you did towards others. This will do wonders to your soul.

Eternal Progress Open to every Human Soul

In most people, there is an ingrained desire to make some kind of progress with their life. Moreover, every human being has the innate ability and power to spread not only their wisdom, but also their love. And this can be achieved regardless of who that person is. Everybody has the ability to work towards wisdom and understanding regardless of their walk of life. There is a direct relationship between desire for mental and spiritual understanding and rate of progress. And as we have already mentioned, our soul will continue to exist long after our physical body does not. The path for progress will always be open and we are able to walk it at any time. Which ultimately, can help with many of the challenges that are happening within the world.

How to encompass these in your work

Practice, practice, practice!

You will see this many times throughout this book. The best way to get better at what you do is to get out there and do it.

It might not come easily at first to remember all of these different principles at once. I suggest you write them down in your own words, so you know what they mean to you. From this, you will be able to think about how they map onto your own world.

Reading these principles might mean one thing to you and something else to the person next door. And that doesn't matter. What does matter is what you get from it.

The way you approach all of this is absolutely vital. This isn't about making money or being famous. Being a medium is about serving people and furthering the movement. Remember the people we looked at in the Introduction? These were all people who wanted to help the movement and help other people. Approach all of this with the same deals and you will be in the best position to become a freestyle medium.

Think about each of these principles when you are sitting with people. They will form the cornerstone of the words that come out of your mouth. For example, the continuous existence of the human soul is an integral part of the conversations you have with people. Your evidence is all part of providing proof of this. Without this principle in your heart, the way you discuss with people might not carry the same weight or have the same impact.

We will touch upon these again throughout the book as we

look at how you become the medium you are meant to be. Evidence and trust are rooted deep in these principles so make sure you read this chapter at least a couple of times and digest the information. It will help you to develop your skills and keep you on track.

As with all of this, if you have any questions then look at the rest of this book as well as speaking to other mediums. Don't be overly swayed by the opinions of others but use them as a resource to question and test your beliefs.

CHAPTER 4

INTELLIGENCES OF THE SPIRIT WORLD

LOOKING A LITTLE DEEPER AT WHAT HAPPENS

Looking a little deeper at what happens

Brahmakumari Shivani provides a good definition of spiritual intelligence. Which is "expression of inner spiritual qualities which are conveyed through your thoughts. As well as actions & attitude". However, it is possible to extend this definition further. Specifically, into the areas of being spiritual. And having intelligence.

Being spiritual is all about interacting. As well as thinking & acting within your spirit. Rather than your physical self. During our lifetime, we tend to have labels thrown on us. Such as race, gender & nationality. However, this is an incorrect way to view ourselves. According to the rules of spirituality. Which can potentially lead to negative emotions, such as fear, anger & sadness. Moreover, such emotions can lead to misidentification. Which distracts an individual from being their true self.

The other definition we need to look at is intelligence. Which means using your knowledge at the right time. As well as in the right way & place. And with the correct intention. Do you view yourself as a spiritual person? If you are, you will be aware that nothing in life is owned. As such, damaged or lost objects in your life should not affect you. Instead, the spiritual power within you allows acceptance & moving on. e.g. If someone makes a negative comment about your appearance. As a spiritual person, you should not be affected. True beauty does not lie in appearance. Instead, it lies within character & nature. As such, things should allow you to keep calm under negativity. Our spirit provides us strength. And this strength can be drawn out of us. And used as & when needed.

So, what is the difference between spiritual intelligence & spirituality?

Spirituality tells you who you are. Whereas spiritual intelligence allows you to realise who you are. And achieved through daily reflection. It is true to say that you have to be true to who you are. It is not possible to be anyone else. The sooner you realise this, the better you feel. Spirituality allows you to gain a higher understanding of yourself. Either as a spirit or a soul. As well as the best understanding of spiritual qualities & attributes. Including love, peace, purity & bliss. Such qualities can be further expressed through thoughts, actions & behaviour. Spirituality removes issues associated with ego. Helping re-develop virtue of character.

Spirituality allows you to connect your inner body with the outside world. And identifies all humans as separate spirits. It is important to dissociate with constructed identities, for example, gender. Spirituality allows us to develop inner peace. And allows you to gain a better understanding of who you are. And your true nature. It also helps with the removal of conflicted inner identities. Once you manage to do this, you develop your own inner world. Rather than being dictated with the world. As such, the world cannot impose things on you. Your own identity already dictates this. Allowing you to shape & develop your own world.

Why is spiritual intelligence interesting?

<u>Did you know that emotional & spiritual intelligence interact?</u>

It is possible to develop a higher level of emotional literacy & intelligence. Which can be achieved by better understanding your own feelings & emotions. Many people believe that emotions are caused by outside events, or the actions of others. However, this is not the case. We are only responsible for our own emotions. We can further develop our spiritual intelligence. Which can be achieved by further understanding the origins of our emotions.

There is a difference between rational & emotional intelligence. Rational intelligence allows us to manage information. Using emotions such as logic & analysis. In contrast, emotional intelligence allows us to control & understand our emotions. And become better attuned to the feelings of others. Spiritual intelligence allows us to use the resources within us. Allowing us to tolerate & care for others. And also adapt our own lives. Along with helping us develop a stronger sense of identity and form better relationships. Spiritual intelligence allows you to align your own personal values. With a clear sense of purpose. And stronger sense of integrity. Allowing you to live by your own values with no compromise.

Most people are motivated by factors outside their own being. However, motivation within us is much stronger. Our own thoughts & values should ultimately motivate us. In addition to the use of our own memories. However, strong sense of purpose is a large motivator. As is a strong sense of meaning. Ultimately, the crossover of emotional & spiritual intelligence manifests itself. When we become aware of who we are. In addition to where we are & what we have in our life. This allows us to develop better self-awareness. And furthermore, enables us to develop a true meaning of certain circumstances and events.

What is the difference between a spiritual quest & a quest from god? Is spirituality a search for truth & peace in ourselves rather than from god? Does spirituality occur within us rather than in the outside world?

The process of spirituality is highly personal. And furthermore, requires a deep connection with god. The main problem is that some of humanity believe that god is only a concept. And as such, people will struggle to create a relationship with something non-existent. The way to progress is to view god as being real. Which allows you to establish a relationship with him. Around the principles of purity, love & peace. Such principles can be seen in the relationship between a child & parent. And if a parent doesn't exercise these principles, a connection cannot be established, despite being a fundamental part of the person within. We should attempt to develop a strong relationship with god. Helping us develop a better knowledge of ourselves. However, spirituality is not all about searching for god. Instead, it is an embodiment of love & peace. And having a strong relationship with god. As such, spirituality allows us to charge the 'battery of the soul'. However, god is the one providing the power.

What can you do with spiritual intelligence?

Did you know that spiritual intelligence can be used practically, day to day?

Spiritual intelligence allows us as humans to gain a better understanding of others. At a much deeper level. It allows us to understand the behaviour of other people. Without passing judgement. And can help us to help others meet their own personal needs. However, you should also aim to meet your own needs. It is true to say that attachment & neediness can become a problem in our family lives. Here, we provide some hints & tips of how this can be reduced:

In our personal lives, it is possible to reduce neediness or clinginess in relationships. We already have things such as love & happiness within us. and in most relationships, there is no real agenda. Because of this, it is possible to develop better relationships. As long as trust and respect are there.

In our family lives, we can develop a high level of familiarity within our family unit. Which can cause negative behaviours. e.g. rejection, resistance & dependency. By improving spiritual intelligence amongst family members, we learn how to relate better. Helping to reduce dependencies on others. As well as accepting other people. Regardless of emotions and behaviours being used.

It is possible to develop better spiritual intelligence at work. Allowing us to no longer see work as a chore. Or to make money. Instead, we may view work as providing a valuable service. We start to treat our fellow colleagues as people rather than objects used to get the job done. And the enhanced relationships we develop at work carry transferable skills into other relationships. Developing trust, integrity & empathy. We may also be able to develop leadership skills. With a proactive attitude & positive vision. Improving our ability to keep calm during periods of chaos.

In my experience, spiritual intelligence can mean a lot of things to a lot of people. I spoke with someone once at a sitting and all I got from her was the word, "no." She didn't recognise anything I was saying to her. None of the information was resonating with her at all.

I asked her to go away with the information and to check it. I asked her to speak to members of her family and ask them if it meant anything. I also told her that she could have her money back if she went away, checked and it didn't mean anything. She came back to me a short time later to confirm that the information was correct and was indeed relevant to her and her life.

Simply put, she wasn't ready to receive the information. She wasn't in the right place to hear what was being said and match it to her own world.

That happens sometimes. It's all about the way the spirit world works with intelligence that makes a massive difference to what is going on.

Is it possible to develop a higher level of spiritual intelligence?

Misconceptions & illusions are the only barriers that limit you to developing a higher level of spiritual intelligence - blocking the path to be your true self. And being true to who you are. As you begin to remove these obstacles, you gain better realisation. And improved spiritual intelligence. There are a number of ways this can be achieved. Such as:

Meditation. Meditation allows you to learn more about yourself. And become more self-aware. It develops the ability to better control your own thoughts & feelings. And separate truth from illusions. Allowing you to ultimately make better, more intelligent choices.

Detached observation. This describes disengagement with action and interaction that happens outside our body. Specifically, disengaging with current thoughts. This doesn't mean avoiding situations. Rather better understanding of what is happening around us. And not wasting our mental energy on unimportant things. As ultimately, this is where tiredness originates from.

Reflection. Reflective time every day is important to look back at the interactions we have been involved in. And help us to understand the consequences of our actions.

Connection. Connection provides the ultimate source of spiritual power. Helping to improve spiritual intelligence. By utilising inner energy from the supreme source, we can begin to clear the inner clutter. And better focus on our own consciousness.

Practice. Unless you make changes in your life, you will not be able to progress further. In terms of your spiritual development. And develop new behaviours. As such, you must continually engage in new learning. To gain new insight & realisation.

Seeing. It is essential to always try & see the best in others. And encourage them to be the best they can be. As such, it is important to make sure that you express positivity.

Looking a little deeper at what happens here

Every person has free will. They are sent down to the earth perfect in every way in terms of the soul. Any physical differences such as illness are something different – the soul is the part of you that is sent to this world in perfect shape. The soul is vitally important to all that we do. If we are true of heart, then we can be the right person for our life. The soul is the part of you that lives before you are born and lives on after you pass away. It is this part of you that the medium can connect with via their guide in the afterlife. From there, you can stay connected to those that you love.

You make all of the decisions that affect your life with the spirit of free will etched onto your very essence. There are no decisions that are already made that you cannot influence. This is the free will that many talk about – it exists. There are consequences to our decisions, but we are free to make any decision that we like. And it is the same in the spirit world. The spirits have total free will. They cannot be prompted or bribed to help you. They will not be bullied into revealing things that are out there just because you want to know them. Working with a spirit guide is about treating them with respect and understanding. This is just as it would be with anyone else you encounter – especially someone that you want to help you.

There are certain reasons why you wouldn't be able to work with a spirit guide and be able to produce a reading for someone. It is really interesting at this point of the book to consider these. You have read a large portion of this book and are probably now really interested in becoming a freestyle medium. But these are very early days. There is a lot to be learned. Hearing that there might be times when you could struggle to get a reading right here, right now will help you to understand that you will need to work on this constantly to get the most from it.

Here are some of the main reasons why a medium might not be able to gain a reading –

The medium doesn't have enough experience

There you go, we've said it! Not being experienced enough means that you make mistakes. It is the same with anything new that you learn. The first time you learned to swim, there will have been times when you were not moving through the water quickly enough. You will have been taking it easy and not kicking your legs or moving your arms in the same manner or at the same rate you did when you were practicing. You will have done something that is pretty much the opposite of swimming – you will have been sinking. It is then time to go back to basics, check over all you have been taught and try again.

There is no difference with being a medium, especially a freestyle medium. Like a freestyle swimmer, there is a certain degree of looseness about what you do. Following the rules and structures given to you by someone else doesn't allow you to become the medium you are meant to be. But forgetting all of the ideas you developed at the beginning (especially those that you put together while reading this book) can lead you to miss out on readings.

Taking that step back and acknowledging this is the sign of an experienced medium. You might be tempted to struggle on. You might be tempted to push through a reading when one doesn't exist. Don't be tempted to do either of these. Just relax and chalk it up to experience. We all get things wrong from time to time, I am living breathing confirmation of this, and we should just accept that it builds us into a better medium in the long run.

The one thing you need to bear in mind with all of this is that you don't let your ego get in the way. As with many things in life, you will want to be a successful medium as soon as you possibly can. This just isn't practical. Sit in front of a piano for the first time, and nobody expects you to be a concert pianist – least of all yourself. You might be tempted to exaggerate your piano skills in front of friends from time to time as you learn more and become better at it. But the way you are with the piano will remain the same – you don't get better by simply pretending you are better. The same goes for your mediumship. You shouldn't let your ego get in the way and try to be all things to all people. You will know certain things at the beginning and your skills in this area will improve over time. But be honest with other people – and be brutally honest with yourself. If you can't connect then let the person sat with you that you can't connect. Integrity and reputation mean a huge deal in mediumship so don't sell yourself short by filling in the blanks in your skills with your ego.

And this links to the next reason...

The medium works on fear

Before you go any further, don't worry. This is nowhere near as frightening as it sounds. Working on fear means that the medium doesn't trust themselves enough at that point in time to get a good reading. As with the above, an inexperienced medium will not have developed the skills to be able to deal with all situations that they encounter. And the medium will know this too.

Don't be afraid that you haven't dealt with every possible situation yet. None of us can know what comes around the next corner. None of us know what will happen at the next reading. Being fearful that you might not be able to perform is a scary place to be. You start to close your eyes and focus on the potential that you might get something wrong.

It is the same with so many things in life. Focusing on the fear of all the things that can go wrong taints our mind. Our thoughts become negative. We are asking the universe to bring us these. When we focus on the positive side of life then everything feels so much better. We don't worry about what might go wrong but instead start to be happy about all of the things that can go right!

Sending out negative thoughts and having a closed mind to the positive side of life can have a large impact on the mediums ability to get a reading. Like the above reason, the medium than starts to wonder if they have the ability at all. They think that they need to do something different or even give it up totally. Don't put yourself in this situation. Just relax and know that you can do this!

Think positive and positive things will happen. We are here to ensure that we can support others in their journey. Don't stop because you are fearful of failure. Turn that round and become excited about your success.

The medium doesn't have enough life experience

It is a fact of life that we gain experience as we get older. Being younger isn't a barrier to becoming a great freestyling medium, it does leave you in a position where you may have amassed less life experience than other mediums. Life experience means a lot to a medium. It gives them the ability to relate to the people they communicate with both in the spirit world and on planet earth. Being connected to others, understanding their world view and communicating adapts the way that you make things work as a medium.

Why this is interesting for your freestyle mediumship

To begin with, everything you do as a medium and as a person is interesting. Don't ever lose sight of that fact.

But on a deeper level, this is all part of a journey. There isn't a beginning as such because you are already on the path whether you know it or not. There isn't an ending because you will be learning for the rest of your life and then beyond that as well. But there is a middle – and that's the bit we are all at now.

If you open your ears, your heart and your mind to the world around you then you can develop a whole lot quicker than with all of these closed to the world. Becoming the best freestyle medium you can be is all about realising that you don't have all the answers today, tomorrow, next week, in 3 months' time or in 5 years. You will get more answers as time goes on but thinking that you know all there is to know is a dangerous place to be.

So, open your mind to the certainty that you will learn more every day about the spirit world, about your skills as a medium and about life itself. That's a certainty, remember.

Your mind is the first thing you should open every day of your life. Once this is open and ready, you can get on with everything else you need to move forward.

The fascination with everything that goes on around you in the world is a powerful thing that will help you to become a great learner. There are not many people in the world that would describe themselves as a great learner first and foremost. But it is a wonderful thing to be.

There is a whole world out there, literally, that you can learn about. Closing your mind the day you leave school, and deciding that your learning is over because you are not assigned a teacher is a crazy way to live your life. You are, in fact, assigned a teacher. It's just not in the way that you or society readily accepts.

Your teacher is your spirit guide and they will be there for you along the way. Accept their teachings and work with them to become someone who develops and gets better at what they do every day.

What you can do with it

My word, this can take you a long way. Your intelligence is something that you may not want to talk about openly. We have built this society where people are either seen as intelligent or not. We are told by those in power that there are certain things we must do in order to be considered intelligent.

And many of us don't think that we fit into this category.

But there are different intelligences. And the basic level of intelligence isn't one that brings us a stack of qualifications from school. It is one that brings us closer to the spirit world.

You should consider your place in the biggest picture of all. When I was at school, there was no way I thought I could ever write a book. If someone had told me that I would become an author in my life I would have laughed at them – and so would my teachers!

But the intelligence I have developed in my time as a medium has brought me to this point. I am now in a place where I can bring a lot of this intelligence together and share it with the world. And I am happy to do this.

Your intelligence level may not be what the other pupils in school thought fitted their definition of 'intelligence.' But you are your own judge of this now. You are in the position where you can decide what works for your life.

Think about what this means and where you want it to take you. Applying the teachings of this book in the world will give you the ability to connect to others and become someone who is trusted. But in addition to that, you will also become someone who is respected for your intelligence. The spiritual intelligence that you have now and the spiritual intelligence that you will develop over the coming days, weeks, months and years will open doors for you. It will change your life.

But you need to embrace the way the world sees spiritual intelligence for the positive. There may be a few negative people out there but listen to the positive messages and build on this to become a freestyle medium.

You should get into the intelligences of the spirit world by listening to the signs that are all around you. One of the main things you can do is to learn about the Chakras and what they mean to you. We'll take a look at that next.

The 7 Chakras

Energy in the universe exists with abundance. However, this is also true of the human body and all living things. The 7 chakras describe this energy.

A literal translation of 'chakra' is 'wheel'. This is because the energy within you is continuously spinning. Each type of energy describes from the top of your head right down to the bottom of your spine. And can furthermore be divided into 7 types.

These chakras are well balanced in individuals experiencing good health. Enhancing mind, body and spirit. However, health problems can occur when these are spinning at the incorrect speed.

By expanding your knowledge of the 7 chakras, you can align yourself better with the natural energy cycles of your body.

By correcting these imbalances, you can begin to repair spiritual, physical and emotional imbalance. Helping your health to improve and your ability to live a life of harmony.

What role do they play in my life?

Each chakra has a specific location within your body. Along with an important purpose. As such, if a chakra is out of balance, you may experience specific symptoms. Which is why we also explain how to heal such chakras. So, what are the different types of chakra and where are they located?

Root Chakra - Muladhara

This chakra takes its name from the word 'Mula', meaning root and Dhara which refers to support. As such, this chakra is all about connecting your energy with the Earth. Also known as grounding. This is referring to the energy you need day to day to survive on this Earth. Particularly security over finances and emotions.

Where is this chakra located? The very bottom of your spine close to your tailbone and just below the belly button.

How will I know if this chakra is balanced? You will experience a feeling of peace and accomplishment with regards to subjects such as safety, shelter and finances. Moreover, you will feel better connected as a human being.

How will I know if this chakra is overactive? This chakra can become overactive. And lead to symptoms such as anxiety. In reality, there is probably no real threat. Physical symptoms can include digestive issues, back/hip pain and cysts for women or prostate issues for men.

How can I balance my chakra? First of all, make sure that you are making effective use of the energy given off by this chakra. Then begin to calm the chakra by improving your spiritual connection through praying and meditating. Alternatively, think about volunteering or completing acts of kindness. This helps remove overactivity from this chakra, moving it into other energy centres.

How can I tell if my chakra is underactive? If you already take good care of your survival needs, chances are, you haven't had much opportunity to fully activate this chakra throughout your life. And this may present its self as daydreaming, concentration problems or a feeling that your head is 'in the clouds'.

How can I energise this chakra? Being out in nature is sufficient for this. E.g. gardening, swimming or walking in the forest.

Sacral Chakra - Svadhishana

The translation of this chakra is "the place of the self". i.e. What your identity is and what you do with this.

This chakra is all about enjoying life. Which is provided through a creative life force energy. This energy allows you to reap what you sow. Allowing you to take part in activities that bring you pleasure in life.

Where is this chakra located? Just below the belly button.

How will I know if this chakra is balanced? You will probably be making the most of the pleasurable things in life. And ultimately, you will experience feelings of wellness from them.

How will I know when this chakra is overactive? This chakra is likely to be overactive when you are overindulging on things or have an addiction. Nevertheless, you should not feel bad when you make use of the good things life has to offer. Apart from indulging in things that are particularly bad for you.

If you are overweight, feel restless or addicted to something, this could indicate that this chakra is overactive.

How can I balance this chakra? If you feel this chakra is overactive, this symptom can be reduced by drawing more energy into your heart. Furthermore, before each adverse action you take, make sure to question yourself whether the activity is beneficial for you.

How can I tell if this chakra is underactive? This chakra can become underactive if you spend frequent amounts of time in life on practical things without actually enjoying life. Symptoms that this may be true include lack of creativity, reduced passion and depression.

How can I energise this chakra? Fortunately, the answer to this is rather easy... just have fun and enjoy your life. Make sure that you take time out and enjoy yourself.

Solar Plexus - Manipura

This type of chakra means "lustrous gem"'. Which is the location where your identity, self-confidence and power originate from. Being in certain situations in life and knowing intuitively they are not right for you can commonly lead to a feeling in your gut.

Where is this chakra located? In the middle of the belly button which extends up the breastbone. Or where both sets of ribs connect at the middle of your chest.

How do I know if this chakra is balanced? You will experience a feeling of personal power, wisdom and decisiveness. Another term for this chakra is the 'warrior chakra'. Which refers to a warrior heading into battle.

How can I tell if this chakra is overactive? One possible sign is when our power infiltrates into the lives of others. Symptoms may include feeling angry, lack of empathy or the urge to micromanage people at work. Other issues can include digestive problems or issues experienced in other bodily organs.

How can I balance this chakra? Balancing this chakra is all about practising love and kindness. Try some meditation, encouraging your love and kindness to all those around you.

How can I tell if this chakra is underactive? This often occurs when we lack personal power which can drain us of energy. This may result in symptoms such as being timid, neediness and feeling insecure.

How can I energise this chakra? This can be achieved by thinking about everything you are good at and practising your talents. This will lead to a tingling and vibrating feeling in your stomach.

Heart - Anahata

This type of chakra means 'unhurt'. This chakra is the centre of feelings such as kindness, love and compassion. Not only for other people but also for yourself. As such, there is a strong association of health and wellbeing with this chakra.

Where is this chakra located? Your heart. Extending down to your breastbone and up to your throat.

How do I know if this chakra is balanced? This will appear as a feeling of love. Not only for others but also for yourself. It will be possible to see kindness and compassion in others, even during difficult periods.

How can I tell if this chakra is overactive? You are likely to be making unhealthy choices and may start to lose personal boundaries. Treating yourself with compassion and kindness is vitally important. However, you should never put others needs before your own. So, if you are experiencing symptoms such as a fast heartbeat, problems with relationships or even heartburn, make sure to check this.

How can I balance this chakra? This can be achieved by merely spending some more love on yourself than you give to others. More specifically, try and do one thing per day that you enjoy.

How can I tell if this chakra is underactive? Having an underactive chakra of this type is relatively common. Heartbreak in life has a purpose. To show us a lesson not only about ourselves but the world around us. When this type of chakra is underactive, you may feel it is difficult to get too close to people. Which can manifest as circulatory problems.

How can I energize this chakra? Energizing this chakra can be challenging. As over time, we have built our guard up high. However, to begin this process, you need to start by loving and appreciating yourself.

Throat - Vishuddha

This type of chakra is also known as 'Vishuddha' meaning 'very pure'. And it helps you in voicing personal truths. The throat allows you to do this. However, this chakra allows you to clearly state the truth, using internal energy. Located just above the heart, it connects the compassion and love for other people and you.

Where is this chakra located? Between your collarbone. It also moves down centre to your heart right through to the centre of your eyes.

How do I know if this chakra is balanced? Your expression will be conveyed with kindness, truth and love. Your choice of words will always be appropriate, regardless of the situation. If this chakra is balanced, you will have the power to inspire and enlighten everyone around you.

How can I tell if this chakra is overactive? One common reason this happens is when you are failing to make yourself heard. As such, if you continually interrupt others and love the sound of your own voice, this chakra could be overactive. You may also experience mouth ulcers and throat pain.

How can I balance this chakra? Fortunately, balancing this chakra is easy. Simply think before you speak! Ask yourself whether what you are about to say is necessary, sincere and kind.

How can I tell if this chakra is underactive? An individual consistently being ignored may react with silence. Or maybe described as being shy or struggle to reveal their emotions. The individual might experience digestive issues. Due to energy being sent to the 3rd chakra.

How can I energize this chakra? Be honest and practice emotional expression with yourself. We are taught only to speak the truth when people are around to hear it. However, you can still energize this chakra by doing this.

The third eye - Anja

Also meaning 'beyond wisdom', this chakra goes beyond all senses and the material world. Allowing you to develop better perception, psychic energy and intuition. In our brain, there is a gland which helps determine whether it is day or night as a result of measuring light levels around us.

Therefore, going beyond what the existing five senses can measure.

Where is this chakra located? This chakra is located in between your eyebrows. And it extends between your mouth and the top of your head.

How do I know if this chakra is balanced? You will begin to feel connected with the material and physical world. You will also be able to frequently receive psychic information from all physical senses.

How do I know if this chakra is overactive? The likelihood of this is extremely low. As most of us are in touch enough with the physical world. This chakra can become overactive if you overly engage with activities such as tarot readings or astrology. Which can distract you from day to day living.

How can I balance this chakra? Just remind yourself that you are an earthly creature. And as such, try and do activities that connect you to the Earth such as walking along a beach or digging in your garden.

How can I tell when this chakra is underactive? This is relatively common. The world sometimes discourages the development of our own intuition. And the ignoring of our psychic experiences. Making us feel disconnected. Resultantly, you may develop allergy problems and headaches.

How can I energize this chakra? This takes practice. Try and complete quiet meditation and be aware of signals outside your body. Listen to your spirit. This makes it easier to connect with your 3rd eye. And energy given out here.

Crown - Sahasrara

This means 'thousand-petaled' which also means pure conscious energy. The type of energy given off by this chakra can be challenging to describe. However, magnetism is one concept it can be compared to. When you hold two magnets together, you can feel the force between them. However, this force cannot be seen. This is similar to conscious energy. And this exists everywhere. Helping human beings to connect to the whole universe. The energy given out by this chakra is a reasonably universal energy rather than something personal.

Where is this chakra located? The centre of this chakra is located at the top of your head. It exists between your eyes then extends upwards and outwards. The energy connects you to the entire universe.

How do I know if this chakra is balanced? Achieving balance for this chakra is not easy. It is comparable to achieving nirvana in Buddhism. Which can be compared to overcoming suffering and death, amongst other things. However, it isn't the final outcome. Instead, the process of working towards it that enhances health, happiness and wisdom. Ultimately, it also allows you to balance other chakras in the process.

How do I know if this chakra is overactive? Having an overactive chakra of this type is not possible. It is a universal source of energy.

How can I balance this chakra? There is no need to work out how this can be reduced because this chakra cannot become overactive.

How can I tell when this chakra is underactive? If you have an underactive chakra, this indicates that you are in fact a human being! However, if you would like to enhance the energy of this chakra, practice spiritual development and balancing of other chakras.

How can I energize this chakra? Rather than trying to activate this chakra, you should try and balance your other chakras. To make the most of this chakra, make sure to meditate and connect with spirits. As well as enjoying every day. It is comparable to attempting to winning an Olympic gold medal. Rather than focusing on the end goal, you should instead do the appropriate training for mind and body first. Ensuring good balance within all your body.

As you can see, the chakras are important to your mental, physical and spiritual wellbeing. Make sure you are mindful of these as you work and the results will be beneficial to your journey as a freestyle medium.

CHAPTER 5

THE CLAIRS

WHAT THEY ARE

What are they?

In a nutshell, the Clairs are powerful tools used by mediums to connect with the spirit world and bring forward evidence of a loved one's presence there.

Much like our senses are used to perceive and understand the world around us, mediums use extrasensory perception to perceive and understand the spirit world (extra senses!). Mediums act as a vessel between spirits and human beings and their job is to interpret messages from spirits to the best of their ability and pass these on to their loved ones.

Four are most commonly used within Mediumship.

Typically, a medium will use their strongest couple of Clair senses, but may possess them all (all being around eight in total) There are four main Clairs mainly used within the practice of Mediumship, and depending how the spirits wish to communicate, each Clair can be received in different ways.

Clairvoyance – The power to clearly see the spirit world.

This may be through symbols, figures or images, either externally (with their own eyes) or internally (within the mind). These images will be three-dimensional, telling a story of something which happened either a long time ago or is yet to happen.

- **Clairaudience** - The power to clearly hear the spirit world
- This may be through words, sounds, music and voices, either externally (with their own ears) or internally (within the mind).
- **Clairsentience** - The power to clearly feel the spirit world.
- This may be through feelings, emotions, empathy or physical sensations like feeling your hair grow or a pain in your chest.
- **Claircognizance** - The power to clearly (just know!) something about the spirit world, without logic or facts.

And the rest...

In addition to the four main Clairs there are four others which may be used.

- **Clairempathy** (the power to emotionally feel the spirit world)
- **Clairgustance** (the power to taste something the spirit world wants you to taste without putting anything in your mouth, for example chocolate cake, a loved one's favourite food)

- **Clairtangency** (the power to gain knowledge of the past or future through touching an object of historical significance)
- **Clairsalience** (the power to smell something the spirit world wants you to smell without the subject being there, for example the perfume or cigar smoke of a loved one).

They can be developed.

Mediums must develop all eight Clair senses in order to provide both the fullest experience possible, and to be able to translate messages from the spirit world most accurately. They can do this by focusing on the following.

- Building upon their knowledge of what things look, sound, taste like etc. so they are able to translate messages most accurately. Much like when you are learning a foreign language, you are continually exposing yourself to new vocabulary.
- Developing themselves as human beings, so that they are in a good, strong place. This way their own emotions will not interfere in the process.
- By shutting off distracting senses, they can bring each sense to the forefront and give it their full focus. For example, to improve Clairsentience you can place cotton wool in your ears and a blindfold over your eyes.

How can the Clairs help people?

As well as providing a thrilling and entertaining experience during a one-to-one reading or floor event, a medium's Clairs can also help people deal with the loss of loved ones. This will always be a large part of the work you carry out as a medium. People want to be connected to loved ones and to feel in some way that they are still a large part of their life.

The evidence of the survival of loved ones within the spirit world, brought forward by mediums through the Clairs is sometimes so personal and unique that people feel it must be true. It brings comfort to people who have lost someone they loved, reassuring them that their loved ones are still with them. Information picked up by the Clairs can help guide them to move forward with their lives and help them to heal their grief which may have been creating physical or mental discomfort.

Reading the Clairs is a lost art in many ways. They should be something you want to be a part of and feel like are a part of you. Being able to use the Clairs in your work will help you become a better freestyle medium. The more you work with them, the more confident you will become.

The word Clair means 'clear' in French. So, you will understand that all of this is centred around being clear with your senses. For example, clairvoyance means 'clear seeing.' To make all of this happen you need to be in that calm and relaxed state. Having clear senses means letting the messages sent by the spirit world come through. I'm sure at first you think that these might come solely from sound. We think that the spirit world will talk to us all the time and let us know what is happening with their voice. But that isn't always the case. Be open-minded enough to consider that the messages may come from sounds, smells, touch and taste as well. The freestyle medium must know that there are other ways in which their spirit guide can assist them. You should be open enough in all of your senses to take in this information, while remembering that some of the Clairs are subconscious as well.

WHAT THEY MEAN TO PEOPLE

What do they mean to people?

Believing that the information provided through the Clairs is evidence your loved one is in the spirit world is a powerful tool in itself.

The people that you sit with will want to know as much information as you can give them. Letting them know that someone has said something is one thing. Adding in the tastes, sounds, smells and feelings that go with this as well as the subconscious stuff will make the whole experience far more real for the person who is sat opposite you.

Imagine how much more powerful your message if you were able to talk about the smells you were experiencing when connecting with your spirit guide. They will evoke strong memories for the person you are working with. They will strengthen your evidence no end and put you in a position where you will be far more believable as a medium.

And that is one of the most important reasons to be aware of the Clairs and open to their power. If you can become more confident in what you do (and, in turn, allow others to be more confident in you) then you can explore more and more of what the spirit world has to offer you. Being a freestyle medium is an amazing feeling. It's something I am thankful for every day of my life. And you can have this too!

The Clairs are therefore important, because they allow people the chance to say goodbye to their loved ones (especially if they were not able to). They allow messages to be passed to and from the spirit world, so that unanswered questions can be resolved in a person's mind for example that their loved one is no longer suffering. All of these things are such a big part of someone's grieving process and can eventually lead to closure.

For those people who are sitting with you, closure can be a massive motivating factor in their life. Not knowing is an unnerving thing. People want some signs that their loved ones are in a good place, whether they believe or not.

And how do you develop them?

The Clairs are an amazing way to connect with the spirit world and give real meaning and evidence to your work. They bring imagery and life to the discussion you have with people.

But they are not totally entrenched in the spiritual world. By this I mean, the more information you have about the world around you, the better you will be able to work with the Clairs.

Start by visualising the world around you. If you are sat at home in the living room reading this then close your eyes. Imagine the way the room is laid out. Think about the position of the chairs, the colours they are in, the way the room flows, any smells you are experiencing, the feel of the fabric and everything else from the room. Accessing the Clairs and expressing them in a way that your audience can understand comes from understanding the world itself. If you don't know what a whistling kettle sounds like, then go and find it out. If you can't remember what freshly baked bread smells like as it comes out of the oven they go ahead and bake some bread. The more you know about the world around you the better you will be able to use the Clairs.

This isn't about vaguely knowing things but being able to recognise the subtle differences in smells, feelings, tastes, etc. Your senses are at the forefront of the Clairs.

There are two main reasons that you want to gain more experience in your knowledge of the world in terms of your freestyle mediumship –

1. Your spirit guide will be able to work with more detail
2. This will help you communicate better with your people

Just looking at something as simple as a noise. The difference between one whistle and another might not mean a great deal to you. But it can transform the level of detail that you can give in your evidence. You will go from perhaps talking about 'a whistle' to being able to clarify that it is a bosun's whistle used in the sea cadets. This will give you so much more credibility with the people sit with. It will turn you from someone vague into someone with a level of detail that impresses.

In terms of my work, I use at least 5 of the Clairs in every sitting, often more. These are all given to me by the spirit world and my guide knows the kind of things I have a great level of detail for. The more time I spend with my guide, the more we can work together to bring about readings that actually have great meaning and depth for my people.

My background is in the medical field, so my guide will show me thing that can look like something out of a medical textbook. This might not mean a thing to many people, but to me it is the perfect way to discuss what is going on. These images work hand in hand with my experience and I am able to translate these into things that my people will understand and engage with.

On one occasion, my guide brought forward a pair of lungs. They looked like a pair of lungs from a medical book, but they were blackened. I immediately understood that the person I was connecting to in the spirit world had most probably died of lung cancer. The more of a knowledge base you can build around yourself, the more you will be able to help people.

But this also goes together with trusting your instincts. The images, sounds, smells and other Clairs that come your way might at first seem like they don't mean a great deal. You may get your conscious brain to take over and push this detail out. But you need to embrace these signs for what they are.

One of the very best ways to do this is to get out there and practice your skills. Offer to work for free with people so you can become a better medium. Explain that it is part of your journey and I'm sure that people will accept your offer. Once you start, accept what is coming to you, try to embrace the Clairs and develop your ability. This is a really exciting time so go ahead and offer to work with people on a free basis. Trust in your vision and make these come true for other people around you.

CHAPTER 6

DEVELOPING YOUR EVIDENCE

THE BENEFITS OF EVIDENCE

The benefits of evidence

There are many people out there who feel that mediumship is something that is 'made up' in order to earn some money. They feel that all mediums are cheats that look for signs given off by the people in their audience and jump on that to give 'a reading' that neither means a great deal nor is individual. If you look at the history of mediumship then you will find many people persecuted for their beliefs and practices in this area. We have moved on somewhat from the days where someone with mediumship skills is labelled a witch, but for some it hasn't moved on very far.

The image of a medium throwing out random names to an audience and then seeing if someone reacts to a vague clue is a large image at the front of the mind of many people in the United Kingdom and beyond.

Quite simply, this is where evidence changes that view.

The evidence that you provide will turn people away from questioning your motives to marvelling at your skills. If you don't provide evidence, then you can be seen as someone who just got lucky when asking a few questions. And that's not what you want for yourself or for others.

Evidence has many benefits, and we will look at these in this part of the chapter –

Belief in what you do from others cannot be underestimated. It is a massive part of gaining the trust of others. And we have already looked at the importance of trust and how it will enhance everything you do. If you give vague comments, then the person you are sitting with won't fully commit to what you are saying. They won't fully believe that you know what you are doing. And without buy-in from people, you won't be able to practice your mediumship with a wider audience. Word of mouth is huge for a medium. People will talk to others and either have positive or negative things to say about the time they spent with you. This isn't comments about you as a person, but about the way you convinced them you were good at what you do or not. And the more negative, the less likely the people they speak to will want to search you out and sit with you. Evidence opens doors in this respect. It allows you to become a better medium because it allows you to speak to more and more people all the time.

Confidence in what you do goes alongside this in many ways. If you sit with more people and give compelling evidence, then you grow in confidence at your ability. I'm sure you have heard of a placebo in medicine. It is a pill that contains no active ingredients and essentially does nothing for the patient in terms of medicine. But, if the people taking this pill believe in it, then there are remarkable medical effects noted. It is the fact that people 'think themselves better.' And you can go a long way on the back of self-belief. It doesn't mean that you are deluded – just that you grow into becoming a medium through the inner strength and belief you can get from giving great evidence.

Stronger ties with your guide are another massive benefit of great evidence that isn't spoken about often enough. The better evidence you are able to gain from your spirit guide, the better you will be able to communicate with them in the future. As with any growing relationship, there are many aspects of your spirit guide that you don't yet know – and them with you. Working on any relationship makes it better. Working on the relationship with your spirit guide is a fascinating journey in itself and the result of this is you becoming a much better medium for the people you sit with.

Communication is essential to becoming a great freestyle medium, as we have already seen in this book. Giving great evidence in the right way is another way to develop better communication skills over time. As you build up your style as a medium, the evidence will work in the best way for the exact person you are delivering it to. Your evidence becomes one of the tools that aid your development over time. Don't underestimate the power of it.

What does undeveloped evidence look like?

The psychic will try to present the connections they make during their connections as their own. There is a certain tone and ring to the words they might use –

I feel that...

I can see that...

I hear...

It is as if they are the ones that is making all of the connections, they are the one that is able to see into the spirit world and gather the evidence needed. But that simply isn't the case. The medium will have a completely different tone, and will use phrases such as –

X tells me...

I am being told by...

I'm sure you can immediately tell the difference between these two sets of phrases. The first is all about the person who is making the connection (the psychic) while the second is all about the spirit guide.

This is also one of the first signs that you are working with someone who doesn't develop great evidence. The fact that they are taking the credit for the work of someone else is a big step in the wrong direction. Then the evidence that follows is vague and doesn't feel right.

The poor examples of psychics have been mocked on TV shows for decades. You will see comedy sketches where the pretend psychic says something like –

"I have the letter P and the colour purple. Does anyone want to take this?"

A flurry of hands will rise (who doesn't have one or the other in their life somewhere, even in the distant past?) and they will work from there. This is poor, generic evidence that anyone could take a guess at.

What does great evidence look like?

Now this is more like it! Looking at the downside of a situation is one thing. Looking at the upside – the positive way in which you can deliver great evidence – is something else altogether.

We have already seen a good example of great evidence above. It goes beyond the vague words that others can pick up on. We looked very early in the book at the difference between a medium and a psychic. Can you remember what that said?

If not, then go back now and refresh your memory. It will help a lot in this section. Bookmark this page and you'll be back here in no time at all, I'm sure.

Are you back? That's great.

Great evidence is the kind of facts that you might be looking for if you need information for a school assignment or to present to your boss at work.

Imagine the situation. You are at work. You need to present something to members of the company in order to secure funding for a specific and exciting project for your department. You start with the words, "I think..."

All the confidence in the room drains away. You are fighting a losing battle. People expected you to have done your research and come back with facts that could be tested and used to make a decision.

Now, think about this in terms of your mediumship. The person you are talking to wants to know something they didn't already know. They want the spiritual equivalent of facts. If you are able to develop evidence that points directly to the person on the other side, then they will instantly warm to you and listen to what you have to say. In addition, you will be able to work with them. Evidence does this. Great evidence does this in spades. Now let's take a look at what great evidence looks like –

Great evidence is detailed. This is the most important thing you should think about when developing your evidence. Anyone can say, "I've got the letter P," and hope that someone bites. This does nothing at all. As we saw in the last section, saying, "I've got your niece and she is showing me the number 4 and the month of December," is precise enough that the person on the mortal side of the equation knows exactly who you are talking about. Removing all of the doubt from the conversation is the ideal way to build an immediate and lasting rapport with someone. This is at the core of your freestyle mediumship. If you build a connection with people, then it becomes far easier for them to open up – and for you to give them something that has a meaning to them. Getting that detail in the early days may not be simple. It may need a lot of questions from you to your spirit guide but taking the time to get it right is absolutely the right way to go.

So, don't be afraid to let people know you might need to ask a few questions of your guide. If they know what is going on, then they will completely understand. Taking time in the beginning puts you in the best place for the long term. You will know what need to ask and how you need to word things in order to get the best result for all concerned.

Great evidence is delivered in the right way. This might sound obvious to begin with, but when you think about the evidence you give, the way in which it is put across can change the way it is received. They say that the responsibility for the understanding of the message lies with the sender and not the receiver. In this instance, once you have the information from your guide, then you are the sender. People will take things in different ways, depending on how you structure it –

"Grandma says hello."

"I have your grandma here and she says hello."

"Would your grandma say hello to you?"

"I have an old lady with grey hair who says hello."

"Hello – that's the first word from your grandma."

"I have an elderly lady with long grey hair, down to her waist with a corned beef pie in her hands and she is saying hello."

All of these are from the same source and can all be said to someone you are sitting with but I'm sure you will agree, they all look different and can be received in a different way.

Much of what you deliver will be in your own style and voice, but you should think about how the words you give will affect the person you are sat opposite.

Great evidence is backed up. Don't think that the time you spend with someone is a one-way conversation. The people you talk to will have questions and you really should have the answers to back up what you say. I have mentioned a few times in this book about filling in the blanks. Don't be tempted to do this. Great evidence is the kind where you have a level of background and detail where you can answer questions about what you have said. People are naturally questioning. They will challenge you (in a nice way) when you have said something. They will test to see if you really know what you are talking about. This is why you should develop great evidence that will help you to enter a conversation with knowledge and confidence that you have the details needed.

CHAPTER 7

WHAT ARE THE NEXT STEPS?

ASSESSING THE PROGRESS MADE WHILE USING THIS BOOK

Assessing the progress made while using this book

The first thing you should do on this journey is take a look back at the steps taken so far. Far too many of us only ever look in the present. We deal with the everyday and consider what is in front of us right now. Hopefully, this book has helped you to look at the future and see where you want to go with your mediumship. If you have an idea of where you want to be, then you can also see where this stacks up against where you are today.

But there is also the past to think about too. The movement in your skills and confidence as a medium will be significant since you started reading this book. Some will have read through the book in only a matter of hours or days, others will have taken weeks or even months over it. That's just the differences in people and the way they process information. However long or short this took, there will always be a development from the start of the book to the finish. There will always be a series of learnings and a set of questions that you want to be answered.

So, you should look back at that period of time and assess the progress you have made. For some, writing this down is a fantastic way to understand the progress made. Grab a pen and paper and make a few notes of your skills, confidence and beliefs now. You can compare these against the ones you had at the beginning of the book if you like.

This book is designed as a guide, so you can develop in your own way. It isn't an instruction manual that tells you to attach part A to part B with part C and then you have the finished article. It is a guide that puts you in the right frame of mind to develop in your own way. There are principles and ideas that you should work to, but apart from that, you are free to make your own decisions, make your own choices and even to make your own mistakes. There is nothing wrong with getting something wrong! It is part of the learning process and will put you in the perfect place to no longer make that mistake in the future.

So, take a little time here and now to think about all of this. This is the point where you look back and consider how this will take you forward.

Building confidence

One of the overriding themes of this book is developing confidence in your freestyling mediumship. If you don't have basic confidence in what you will do, then you can't really develop as quickly.

Now, it sounds simple just saying that you should become confident. If it was that easy, then we would all just be able to flick a switch and become confident.

We all know from our life that it is nowhere near this easy. It takes time.

This is the first thing you should do here.

Tell yourself –

"It takes time. I will get there."

Don't be put off if things don't happen easily to begin with. We have all been through this. Think back to childhood. We didn't come out of the womb able to walk, talk and do all of the other things we take for granted today. It takes some practice and builds over time. Confidence comes from trying something new a few times and then getting it right. Give yourself the credit that you will get there when you have practiced.

To this end, you should look for people who will support you on the way initially. There are support groups that are ready made in the SNU or local spiritualists churches. You will be able to find people online and offline who are interested in the same thing as you. Use these groups to help you build a confidence in yourself and in mediumship as a whole. The more you surround yourself with the right people, the easier it becomes.

They say that you are the sum of the five people you spend the most time with. That means if you spend your time with five negative people, then you will be drawn to negative ideas and thoughts. The opposite also applies – if you spend your time with five super positive people then your outlook on life will be super positive too. So, take a look at the people you spend the most time with. These will help you to become who you will be in the near future. If they are people who share the same beliefs and passions as you, then this will help you on the path to spiritual success.

Using your skills and knowledge

Belief and confidence can only be developed so far by talking to others. The day will come where you have to take theory into practice. I hope that this book has helped you to think about the way you want to be a medium. I have put it together with the sole purpose of building your own style as a medium – which is why the book is called Freestyle Mediumship.

But you will never know what that style is until you have sat with someone and tried to help them. That is the long and short of it.

Until you have practiced your skills, you never know if this is going to be for you and if you are going to enjoy it. Now you have reached a point where you know what it is all about, the next step is to move forward and practice.

I suggest you start by working with people in your life that you know are going to be two things –

1. They are going to be supportive
2. They are going to be honest

If the people you work with in the beginning are not supportive then you can lose your confidence before you even gain it. Being told you are wrong or being told you don't know what you are doing can be quite destructive in the early days. When you get more experienced and the negative voices can be drowned out with a sea of positive experiences. In the early days they can shout really loud. And you also want people who can be honest with you in terms of feedback. Having someone who will give you some pointers in terns of the style, the believability and the confidence is invaluable at this stage – money just can't buy this kind of love.

The more time you spend practicing, the better you get. Don't label it as practice in your mind. It is you developing your skills and assisting others. It isn't play time where you get a free hit at trying to be a freestyle medium. It's a lot of fun, but it's also about taking things seriously. Don't let people down, especially if they are giving up their time to support you.

Looking at where to take this

So, what happens next? Far too many books tell you something and then leave you to it. They just stop (at the end) and think you will pick up the baton and run with it. That's fine for certain subjects, but as far as mediumship is concerned, you want this to continue. A supportive way forward is just the thing you need right now. So, the question comes up –

"Where do I look next?"

The internet is filled with ideas and information about any number of topics. Search mediumship on Google and you come back with around 1.7 million results. Read all of these and not only will you be several decades older, but you will be more confused than ever. Remember, we are looking at freestyle mediumship here – this is the act of being open minded and accepting all of the information we can put our hands on. But the next step after finding information is to take it on its merits. The data you read may or may not fit with your view of the world and the ideas you have begun to develop around being a medium. Think about it and decide whether it helps you on your journey or not.

As part of your development, you will meet other people who are on different stages of a similar journey to you. One of the most exciting parts about developing your mediumship skills is that you will get to talk to others who have the same interests and same passions as you do. Spending time with others who share the same appetite as you for something as fascinating as mediumship is a truly life affirming experience. Speak to people, spend time in their company and, most importantly, listen to what others have to say. The shared experiences, shared knowledge and shared practice is immensely valuable to you as you become the best freestyle medium you can be. But the one thing you need to be careful of is the opinions of others. I have hopefully taught you to be accepting of others and to approach all of this with the most open of minds, if you were not that already. But that doesn't mean you take everything that is said to you as fact. People will say things and you should be in a position to take this on board. But you don't want to be in a position where other people's opinion changes the way you feel. Look deep with this and ensure that you are true to yourself.

Stand by what you are. Don't let other try to persuade you that they know more than you.

P.S. Watch out for the jealousy when you get good. Don't get drawn into battles or negativity. Always remember why you started this.

ACKNOWLEDGMENTS

I'd like to take this opportunity to thank a few people that have been an integral part of my life and my journey as a medium.

I have a lot to thank the following people for in terms of my development as a freestyle medium, and these people have my love and respect –

Natalie Wilkinson

Phillipa Slack

Edith Parish

And, of course, my children are both my reason for doing this and my inspiration.

12046378R00072

Printed in Great Britain
by Amazon